HOW TO PRAY

The Best of
John Wesley
on prayer

BARBOUR
PUBLISHING

ISBN 978-1-60260-014-0

Published by Barbour Publishing, Inc., P.O. Box 719, Uhrichsville, Ohio 44683
www.barbourbooks.com

*Our mission is to publish and distribute inspirational products offering exceptional
value and biblical encouragement to the masses.*

Member of the
Evangelical Christian
Publishers Association

Printed in the United States of America.

introduction

John Wesley was known for many things—his preaching, his writing of books and hymns, his compassion for the poor. He was also famed for his incredible energy: It is said that Wesley rode more than two hundred thousand miles on horseback to preach more than forty thousand sermons. But underlying all of his amazing achievements was his devotion to prayer.

This little book draws from Wesley's many writings—sermons, pamphlets, and books—to provide a glimpse into his heart of prayer. Whether he's actually explaining "the Lord's Prayer" or simply showing the role prayer plays in other areas of life—such as salvation or sanctification—Wesley offers many helpful insights into this most vital of all Christian activities.

"All who desire the grace of God are to wait for it, first, in the way of prayer," Wesley wrote. Prayer is truly, in Wesley's words, "the most useful of all pastimes."

We hope Wesley's insights will prompt you to more frequent, more effective, and more God-honoring prayer.

THE EDITORS

O praise God for all you have and trust Him for all you want!

JOHN WESLEY

what are you *now*?

Examine yourselves to see whether you are in the faith.
2 CORINTHIANS 13:5 NIV

You who are born of God according to the marks laid down in His Word well know that you are His children. Your hearts are assured before Him. Everyone who has observed these marks can sense and know of a truth at this very moment whether, in the sight of God, you are thus His child.

The question is not anything else: What are you *now*? Is the Spirit of adoption *now* in your heart? Make the appeal to your own heart: Are you *now* the temple of the Holy Spirit? Does He *now* dwell within you?

Perhaps you are resting in a transaction made at your baptism, but does the Spirit of Christ and of glory *now* rest upon you, or has the light that was within you become darkness again? To you also I say, "You must be born again." You have read what are the marks of the children of God. All who do not have these on their souls, whether baptized or unbaptized, must needs receive them or without doubt they will perish eternally.

Lord Jesus! May everyone who prepares his or her heart to seek Your face receive that Spirit of adoption and be enabled to cry out, "Abba, Father." Let them now have power so to believe in Your name as to become children of God and know and sense redemption through Your blood and the forgiveness of sins.

the way of prayer

"Pray, then, in this way."
MATTHEW 6:9 NASB

He who best knew what we ought to pray for and how we ought to pray, what matter of desire, what manner of address would most please Himself and best become us, has here dictated to us a most perfect and universal form of prayer. It comprehends all our real wants, expresses all our lawful desires—a complete directory and full exercise of all our devotions. He here directs us to pray *thus*—for these things; sometimes, in these words. At least in this manner: short, close, full.

This prayer consists of three parts—the preface, the petitions, and the conclusion. The preface, *"Our Father who art in heaven,"* lays a general foundation for prayer. It comprises what we must first know of God before we can pray in confidence of being heard. It likewise points out to us the faith, humility, and love of God and man with which we are to approach God in prayer.

"Our Father"—who art good and gracious to all, our Creator, our preserver; the Father of our Lord and of us in Him, Your children by adoption and grace. Not *my* Father only, but the Father of the universe, of angels and human beings. *"Who art in heaven"*—filling heaven and earth and beholding all things in heaven and earth; knowing every creature and all their works, and every possible event from everlasting to everlasting. The Almighty Lord and ruler of all, superintending and disposing all things.

praying for Daily Bread: Food and Grace

"Give us today our daily bread."
MATTHEW 6:11 NIV

The second portion of this prayer consists of six *petitions*, four of which we here consider: "*Hallowed be Thy name*"— may You, O Father, be truly known by all intelligent beings and with affections suitable to that knowledge! May You be duly honored, loved, feared, by all in heaven and in earth, by all angels and all men!

"*Thy kingdom come*"—may Your kingdom come quickly and swallow up all the kingdoms of the earth! May all people receive You, O Christ, for their King and truly believe in Your name. May they be filled with righteousness, peace, joy, holiness, and happiness till they are removed into Your kingdom of glory to reign with You forever.

"*Thy will be done in earth, as it is in heaven*"—may all inhabitants of the earth do Your will as willingly as the holy angels! May these do it continually even as they, without any interruption of their willing service. And, as perfectly as they! O Spirit of grace, through the blood of the everlasting covenant, make them perfect in every good work to do Your will, and work in them all that is well pleasing in Your sight!

"*Give us,*" O Father (for we claim nothing of right; only of Your free mercy) "*today*" (for we take no thought for tomorrow) "*our daily bread*"—all things needful for our souls and bodies, not only the meat that perishes, but the sacramental bread, and Your grace, the food which endures to everlasting life.

Finally, Thine Is the Kingdom

*"For Yours is the kingdom and the power
and the glory forever. Amen."*
MATTHEW 6:13 NASB

Two final petitions: *"And forgive us our debts, as we also forgive our debtors"*—give us, O Lord, redemption in Your blood, the forgiveness of sins. As You enable us freely and fully to forgive, so forgive us all our trespasses.

"And lead us not into temptation, but deliver us from evil"—Whenever we are tempted, O Lord who helps our infirmities, do not allow us to be overcome or suffer loss by it, but make a way for us to escape so that we may be more than conquerors, through Your love, over all sin and the consequences of it.

The principal desire of a Christian's heart is the glory of God (vv. 9–10); and all one wants for himself or others is the "daily bread" of soul and body, pardon of sin, and deliverance from the power of it and of the devil (vv. 11–13). There is nothing besides that a Christian can wish for. Therefore, this prayer comprehends all his or her desires. Eternal life is the certain consequence, or rather completion, of holiness.

The conclusion: *"For Thine is the kingdom"*—the sovereign right of all things that are or ever were created. *"The power"*—the executive power, whereby You govern all things in Your everlasting kingdom. *"And the glory"*—the praise due from every creature for Your power, all Your wondrous works, and the mightiness of Your kingdom, which endures through all ages, even *"forever. Amen."*

The chief of these means [of works of piety] are prayer, whether in secret or with the great congregation; searching the scriptures; (which implies reading, hearing, and meditating thereon;) and receiving the Lord's Supper, eating bread and drinking wine in remembrance of Him: And these we believe to be ordained of God, as the ordinary channels of conveying His grace to the souls of men.

JOHN WESLEY

praying oneself awake

"Awake, sleeper. . .
and Christ will shine on you."
EPHESIANS 5:14 NASB

Discover yourself! If you are one of the poor self-deceivers, awake! Is your confidence a self-confidence that you have the witness in yourself that you are a child of God, and thus defy all your enemies?

Alas! You are weighed in the balance and found lacking. The Word of the Lord has tried your soul and proved it to be reprobate silver. You are not lowly of heart, therefore you have not yet received the Spirit of Jesus. You are not gentle and meek, even tempered. Therefore, your joy is worth nothing; it is not joy in the Lord. You do not keep His commandments; therefore, you do not love Him, nor are you a partaker of the Holy Spirit. It is as certain and as evident as the Word of God can make it: His Spirit does not bear witness with your spirit that you are a child of God.

Cry unto Him that the scales may fall off your eyes, that you may know yourself as He knows you: a poor, undeserving, hell-bound sinner. Pray that you may receive the sentence of death within yourself, until you hear the voice that raises the dead, saying, "Be of good cheer. Your sins are forgiven. Go in peace; your faith has made you whole"; and His Spirit witnesses with your spirit that you are His child.

ask, seek, knock

"Ask, and it will be given to you."
LUKE 11:9 NASB

All who desire the grace of God are to wait for it, first, in the way of prayer. This is the express direction of our Lord Himself. In His Sermon on the Mount, after explaining at length wherein religion consists and describing the main branches of it, He adds, "'Ask, and it will be given to you; seek, and you will find; knock, and it will be opened to you. For everyone who asks receives, and he who seeks finds, and to him who knocks it will be opened'" (Matthew 7:7–8 and Luke 11:9–10 NASB). In the plainest manner, we are here directed to ask in order to receive, or as a means of receiving; to seek, in order to find the grace of God, the pearl of great price; and to knock, to continue asking and seeking, if we would enter into His kingdom.

That no doubt might remain, our Lord gives a peculiar parable of a father who desires to give good gifts to his children, concluding with these words, "'How much more will your heavenly Father give the Holy Spirit to those who ask Him?'"(Luke 11:13 NASB).

Jesus gives a direction to pray, with a positive promise that by this means we shall obtain our request: "'Go into your room, and. . .pray to your Father who is in the secret place; and. . .[He]. . .will reward you openly'" (Matthew 6:6 NKJV).

pray and persevere

> *"Lord, teach us to pray."*
> LUKE 11:1 NIV

Immediately after our Lord answered this request [above] of His disciples, He showed them the absolute necessity of using prayer if we would receive any gift from God.

He told the story of a man who begged his friend at midnight to get up and lend him three loaves of bread. Though the friend would not rise and give him because he was his friend, yet because of his troublesome persistence, his friend will rise and give him. Jesus said, "And I say unto you, Ask, and it shall be given you."

How could our blessed Lord more plainly declare the means—persistently asking—by which we may receive of God what otherwise we should not receive at all?

"He spoke also another parable, to this end, that men ought always to pray, and not lose heart" (see Luke 18:1)— to persevere until they receive of God whatever petition they have asked of Him: *"There was in a city a judge. . .[and] there was a widow in that city; and she came unto him, saying, Avenge me of mine adversary. And he would not for a while: but afterward he said within himself, Though I fear not God, nor regard man; yet because this widow troubleth me, I will avenge her"* (Luke 18:2–5 KJV).

Our Lord Himself made the application for those who cry day and night to Him: "I tell you that he will avenge them speedily" (Luke 18:8 KJV).

prayer Being the cure of Darkness of soul

O LORD. . .examine my heart and my mind.
PSALM 26:2 NIV

To suppose that the cure is the same in all cases is a great and fatal mistake but an extremely common one. The cure of spiritual, as well as bodily, diseases must be as various as the causes of them. The first thing, then, is to determine the cause; this will naturally point out the cure.

For instance: Is it sin which occasions darkness? What sin? Does your conscience accuse you of committing any sin whereby you grieve the Holy Spirit? How can you expect His light and peace should return until you put the thing from you and receive His pardon? Or perhaps it is some sin of omission: Do you reprove those who sin in your sight? Do you walk in the means God has given: public, family, private prayer? If you habitually neglect these known duties, make haste to be no more "disobedient to the heavenly calling." Till the sin, whether of commission or omission, be removed, all comfort is false and deceitful. Look for no peace within till you are at peace with God, which cannot be without fruits suitable to repentance.

Or is there some inward sin which springs up to trouble you? Have you thought more highly of yourself than you ought to think? Have you gloried in anything other than Jesus Christ? Have you ascribed your successes to your own strength, wisdom, or courage? If so, you see the way you are to take: Humble yourself under the hand of God that, in due time, He may exalt you.

Early Morning Prayer

Early will I seek You.
PSALM 63:1 NKJV

How do you begin your day? The generality of Christians, if they are not obliged to work for their living, rise at eight or nine in the morning after eight, nine, or more hours of sleep. I do not say (as I was apt to do fifty years ago) all who do this are in the way to hell. But neither can I say they are in the way to heaven, denying themselves and taking up their cross daily. From more than sixty years' observation, I can say that men in health require an average of six to seven hours of sleep and healthy women from seven to eight each twenty-four hours. This quantity of sleep is advantageous to body and soul, preferable to any medicine I have known, both for preventing and removing nervous disorders. In defiance of fashion and custom, it is, therefore, the most excellent way to take just so much sleep as experience proves our nature to require. It is indisputably most conducive both to bodily and spiritual health.

And why should you not? Because it is difficult? True; with men it is impossible. But all things are possible with God; and by His grace, all things will be possible to you. Only be instant in prayer and it will be not only possible, but easy. And, it is far easier to rise early always than only sometimes. Just begin at the right end: To rise early, you must sleep early. Then the difficulty will cease. Its advantage will remain forever.

All that a Christian does, even in eating and sleeping, is prayer, when it is done in simplicity, according to the order of God, without either adding to or diminishing from it by his own choice.

John Wesley

seeking god

*The blood of Christ, who through the eternal Spirit
offered Himself without blemish to God,
[shall] cleanse your conscience from dead works
to serve the living God.*

HEBREWS 9:14 NASB

Settle this in your heart, that the mere work done profits nothing. There is no power to save but in the Spirit of God, no merit but in the blood of Christ. Consequently, even what God ordains conveys no grace to the soul if you do not trust in Him alone. On the other hand, he that does truly trust in Him cannot fall short of the grace of God, even though he were cut off from every outward ordinance, or shut up in the center of the earth.

In using all means, seek God alone. In and through every outward thing, look only to the *power* of His Spirit, and the *merits* of His Son. Beware you do not get stuck in the *work* itself; if you do, it is all lost labor. Nothing short of God can satisfy your soul. Therefore, fix on Him in all, through all, and above all. For all the power, and all the merit is of Him alone.

Remember also to use all means as *means*—as ordained, not for their own sake, but for the renewal of your soul in righteousness and true holiness. If, therefore, they actually tend to this, that is well; but if not, they are dung and dross.

Have a Holy Urgency

Strive to enter by the narrow door.

Strive, as in an agony of holy fear. A promise has been made of your entering into His rest (see Hebrews 4:9–11). *Strive*, lest you should come short of it.

Strive, in all the fervor of desire, with groans that words cannot express.

Strive by prayer without ceasing. At all times, in all places, lift up your heart to God. Give Him no rest till you, like the psalmist, "awake with God's likeness" and are satisfied with it.

To conclude: *Strive* to enter in at the narrow gate. *Strive*, not only by this agony of soul, of conviction, of sorrow, of shame, of desire, of fear, of unceasing prayer. *Strive*, likewise, by putting in order all your conversation, your whole life, by walking with all your strength in all the ways of God—the way of innocence, of piety, and of mercy. Shun all the appearance of evil. Do all possible good to all people. Deny your own will in all things, and take up your cross daily.

Be ready to cut off everything that would hinder, and to cast it from you. Be ready and willing to suffer the loss of possessions, of friends, of health—of all things on earth—so you may enter into the kingdom of heaven.

wait on the Lord

My soul waits. . .for God only.
PSALM 62:1 NASB

The generality of Christians are accustomed to use some kind of *prayer*. Now, perhaps you are one who still uses the same form you used when you were a child. But surely, there is a "more excellent way" (1 Corinthians 12:31) of ordering our private devotions. Consider both your inward and outward state and vary your prayers accordingly. Suppose you are healthy, at ease, and have kind relations, good neighbors, and agreeable friends. Then your outward state obviously calls for praise and thanksgiving to God.

On the other hand, if you are in adversity, in poverty or need, in distress or danger, or in pain or sickness, then you are called to pour out your soul before God in prayer suited to your circumstances.

In like manner, you may suit your devotions to your inward state, the present state of your mind. Are you in heaviness, either from a sense of sin or from manifold temptations? Let your prayer consist of the confessions, petitions, and supplications that agree with your distressed state of mind.

On the contrary, is your soul in peace? Are you rejoicing in God? Are His consolations large toward you? Then say with the psalmist, "You are my God and I will love You. . .I will praise You." Reading and meditating on a psalm of praise is the natural rising of a thankful heart. "A more excellent way" than any form.

be anxious for nothing

> *"It is your Father's good pleasure*
> *to give you the kingdom."*
> LUKE 12:32 NKJV

How much more, then, will it please our heavenly Father to give us food and raiment? And since you have such an inheritance, regard not your earthly possessions.

To the same effect, the apostle Paul wrote the Philippians (4:6 NKJV): *"Be anxious for nothing, but in everything by prayer and supplication, with thanksgiving, let your requests be made known to God."*

If men are not gentle toward you, yet neither on this nor any other account, be not anxious, but pray. Carefulness and prayer cannot stand together. *"In everything"* great and small, *"let your requests be made known"*; they who by a preposterous shame or distrustful modesty cover, stifle, or keep in their desires, as if they were too small or too great, must be racked with care. But from them they are entirely delivered, who pour them out with a free and filial confidence.

"To God"—it is not always proper to disclose them to people. *"By supplication"*—which is the enlarging upon and pressing our petition. *"With thanksgiving"*—the surest mark of a soul free from care and of prayer joined with true resignation. This is always followed by peace. Peace and thanksgiving are joined together (Colossians 3:15). Thus *"the morrow shall take care for itself"*—be careful for the morrow when it comes. Today, be free from care.

Deny self to obey the Lord

Fervent in spirit. . .
devoted to prayer.
ROMANS 12:11–12 NASB

Here is one who has not made shipwreck of the faith. He still has a measure of the Spirit of adoption, which continues to witness with his spirit that he is a child of God. However, he is not going on to perfection. He is not, as once, hungering and thirsting after righteousness, panting after the whole image and full enjoyment of God as the hart pants after the water brooks (Psalm 42:1). Rather, he is weary and faint in his mind, and, as it were, hovering between life and death.

And why is he thus? Because he has forgotten the Word of God, which says that "*by works faith is made perfect*" (James 2:22). He does not use all diligence in working the works of God. He does not continue instant in prayer—private as well as public. He has slacked off communing at the Lord's Table, or in hearing the Word, in meditation, fasting, and religious conference. If he does not wholly neglect some of these means of grace, at least he does not use them with all his might.

Why does he not now continue in prayer? Because in times of dryness it is pain and grief to him. He does not continue in hearing the Word at all opportunities because sleep is sweet, or it is cold or rainy. So his faith is not made perfect, neither can he grow in grace, because he will not deny himself and take up his cross.

Prayer continues in the desire of the heart, though the understanding be employed on outward things.

JOHN WESLEY

prayer—The crowning weapon

Praying always with all prayer
and supplication in the Spirit, being watchful. . .
with all perseverance. . .for all the saints.
EPHESIANS 6:18 NKJV

The description of the whole armor of God shows us how great a thing it is to be a Christian. The lack of any one thing makes us incomplete. Though one has his loins girded, has on the breastplate, his feet shod, the shield of faith, and sword of the Spirit, yet one more thing is needed: *praying always*. At all times and occasions, in the midst of all actions, inwardly *"praying without ceasing." "By the Spirit"*—through the influence of the Holy Spirit. *"With all prayer"*—all sort of prayer: public, private, mental, vocal. Do not be diligent in one kind of prayer and negligent in others; if we desire our petitions answered, let us use all. Some use only mental prayer, thinking it is a way of worship superior to any other. But it requires far more grace to be enabled to pour out a fervent and continued prayer than to offer up mental aspirations.

"Supplication"—repeating and urging our prayer, as Christ did in the garden; *"watching"*—inwardly attending on God, to know His will, gain power to do it, and attain to the blessings we desire. *"With all perseverance for all the saints"*—continuing to the end in this holy exercise that others may do all the will of God and be steadfast. Perhaps we receive few answers to prayer because we do not intercede enough for others.

always Rejoice;
pray; give Thanks

Rejoice always; pray without ceasing. . .give thanks.
1 Thessalonians 5:16–18 nasb

Rejoice always" in uninterrupted happiness in God. "*Pray without ceasing,*" which is the fruit of "*always rejoicing*" in the Lord. "*In everything give thanks,*" which is the fruit of both the former. *This* is Christian perfection. Further than this we cannot go, and we need not stop short of it.

Our Lord has purchased joy, as well as righteousness, for us. It is the very design of the gospel that, being saved from guilt, we should be happy in the love of Christ.

Prayer may be said to be the breath of our spiritual life. One who lives cannot possibly cease breathing. So much as we really enjoy of God's presence, so much prayer and praise do we offer up "*without ceasing*"; else our rejoicing is but delusion.

Thanksgiving is inseparable from true prayer; it is almost essentially connected with it. One who always prays is ever giving praise, whether in ease or pain, both for prosperity and for the greatest adversity. He blesses God for all things, looks on them as coming from Him, and receives them only for His sake—not choosing nor refusing, liking nor disliking, anything, but only as it is agreeable or disagreeable to His perfect will.

"*For this,*" that you should thus rejoice, pray, give thanks, "*is the will of God,*" always good, always pointing at our salvation!

prayer and grace

You have purified yourselves by obeying the truth.
1 PETER 1:22 NIV

It has been vehemently objected that Christ is the only means of grace. I answer, This is mere playing upon words. Explain your term, and the objection vanishes away. When we say, "Prayer is a means of grace," we understand a channel through which the grace of God is conveyed. When you say, "Christ is the means of grace," you mean the sole price and purchaser of it, that "no man comes unto the Father, but through Him." And who denies it?

But does not the scripture (it has been objected, also) direct us to *wait* for salvation? Does not David say, "My soul waits for God; from Him comes my salvation?" Does not Isaiah teach us the same, saying, "O Lord, we have waited for You"?

All this cannot be denied. We are undoubtedly to *wait* on Him. But how shall we wait? Can you find a better way of waiting for Him than the way He Himself has appointed? Consider the very words of the prophet Isaiah. The whole sentence runs thus: "In the way of Your judgments [or ordinances], O LORD, we have waited for You" (Isaiah 26:8 NKJV). In the very same way did David wait: "Teach me, O LORD, the way of Your statutes, and I shall keep it to the end" (Psalm 119:33 NKJV).

God does nothing but in answer to prayer; and even they who have been converted to God without praying for it themselves, (which is exceeding rare,) were not without the prayers of others.

JOHN WESLEY

ask in faith

Ask in faith without any doubting.
JAMES 1:6 NASB

Regarding the use of prayer as a means of grace, the direction which God has given us by the apostle James is most clear. With regard to prayer of every kind, public or private, and the blessing attached to it, he says: "If any of you lacks wisdom, let him ask of God, who gives to all liberally and without reproach" (James 1:5 NKJV) (if they ask; otherwise "you do not have because you do not ask," James 4:2 NKJV). If they ask, God does not reproach them but says "it will be given to [them]" (James 1:5 NKJV).

Because the apostle adds, "Let him ask in faith," some may object that this is not a direction to unbelievers (to seekers), to those who do not know the pardoning grace of God. I answer: The meaning of the word *faith in this place* is fixed by the apostle himself, as if it were on purpose to halt this objection. The words immediately following are "nothing wavering," *without doubting.* Not doubting but that God hears his prayer and will fulfill the desire of his heart; will grant him the grace, the wisdom for which he asks.

We must conclude, therefore, that scripture shows that all who desire the grace of God are to wait for it in the way of prayer.

family prayer

"Those who are wise will instruct many."
DANIEL 11:33 NIV

We prepare our household to serve the Lord by *instructing* them. We take care to see that every person under our roof has all such knowledge necessary to salvation. It is our responsibility to see that our spouse and children are taught those things which belong to their eternal peace. Plan, especially for the Lord's Day, that all may attend the public services for instruction. And take care that they have time daily for reading, meditation, and prayer. Neither should any day pass without family prayer, seriously performed.

You should particularly endeavor to instruct your children early, plainly, frequently, patiently. *Whenever a child begins to speak*, you may be assured that reason has begun to work. From that time, lose no opportunity of speaking of the things of God.

But speak *plainly*, using such words as little children understand—such as they themselves use. Do this *frequently*, lifting up your heart to God that He would open their understanding and pour His light upon them.

But all this will not avail unless you *persevere* in it. Never leave off till you see the fruit of it. To do this, you will find the absolute need of being endued with power from on high. Without this, I am persuaded, none will have patience sufficient for the work.

Building by prayer and faith

It is with your heart that you believe and are justified.
ROMANS 10:10 NIV

Friend, come up higher! Do not be content with good works: feeding the hungry, clothing the naked, visiting the fatherless and widowed in their affliction, or the sick and those in prison, and the stranger. Do you preach the truth of Jesus in the name of Christ? Do the influence of the Holy Spirit and the power of God enable you to bring sinners from darkness to light, from the power of Satan to God?

Then go and learn what you have taught: By grace you are saved through faith. . .not by our works of righteousness. . .but of His own mercy He saves us (see Ephesians 2:8, Titus 3:5).

Learn to hang naked upon the cross of Christ, counting all you have done just so much dross and dung. Apply to Him just in the spirit of the dying thief and the harlot with her seven devils! *Lord, save or I perish!* Else you are still on the sand; and after saving others, you will lose your own soul.

If you do now believe, pray, *Lord, increase my faith.* Or, if you have not faith, pray, *Give me this faith, though it be as a grain of mustard seed.* For only saving faith, the faith that builds upon a rock, stands firm when the floods rise and the winds blow. And this true saving faith will indeed be manifested in good works of righteousness.

God grant that I may never live to be useless!

JOHN WESLEY

> *"Your Father knows what you need*
> *before you ask Him."*
> MATTHEW 6:8 NASB

In His words just before those above cited, our Lord had been advising against *vain repetition*. Repeating any words without meaning them is certainly vain repetition. Therefore, we should be extremely careful in all our prayers to mean what we say and to say only what we mean from the bottom of our hearts. The vain and heathenish repetitions which we are here warned against are most dangerous, yet very common. This is a principal cause why so many who still profess religion are a disgrace to it. Indeed, all the words in the world are not equivalent to one holy desire. And the very best prayers are but vain repetitions if they are not the language of the heart.

"*And your Father knows what things you have need of.*" We do not pray to inform God of our wants. Omniscient as He is, He cannot be informed of anything which He did not know before. And He is always willing to relieve our needs. The chief thing lacking is a suitable disposition on our part to receive His grace and blessing. Consequently, one great purpose of prayer is to produce such a disposition in us, to exercise our dependence on God, to increase our desire of the things we ask for, and to make us so sensible of our needs that we never cease wrestling till we have prevailed for the blessing (see Genesis 32:24–30).

praying away the darkness

*He does not afflict willingly
or grieve the sons of men.*
LAMENTATIONS 3:33 NASB

Of the various causes of the wilderness state, I *dare not* rank the bare, arbitrary, sovereign will of God, for He rejoices in the prosperity of His servants and delights not to afflict or grieve the children of men. His invariable will is our sanctification, attended with peace and joy in the Holy Spirit. He never desires to withdraw His gifts from us (see Romans 11:29); He never deserts us, as some speak. It is *we who desert Him.*

The most usual cause of inward darkness is *sin* of some kind, *either of commission or omission.* This may be observed to darken the soul in a moment, especially if it is a known, a willful, or presumptuous sin. But light is more frequently lost by giving way to sins of omission. This does not *immediately* quench the Spirit, but gradually and slowly.

The neglect of private prayer, or the hurrying over it, is perhaps the most frequent sin of omission. This lack cannot be supplied by any other means whatever; the life of God in the soul will surely decay and gradually die away.

Another neglect which brings darkness to the soul of a believer is not rebuking a "neighbour" when we see him in a fault but we "suffer sin upon him" (Leviticus 19:17 KJV). By neglecting to reprove him, we make his sin our own. We become accountable for it. By thus grieving the Spirit of God, we lose the light of His countenance.

prayer as a channel of grace

*Grow in the grace and knowledge
of our Lord and Savior Jesus Christ.*
2 Peter 3:18 NIV

The chief of the means of grace are: prayer (whether in secret or in the great congregation); searching the scriptures (which implies reading, hearing, and meditating thereon); and receiving the Lord's Supper (eating bread and drinking wine in remembrance of Him). These we believe to be ordained of God as the ordinary channels of conveying His grace to the souls of men and women.

So it was in the early church. But in process of time, the love of many grew cold. Some began to mistake the means for the end, and to place religion in doing those outward works rather than in a heart renewed after the image of God. Now, the whole value of the means depends on their actually serving the end of religion. Consequently, all these means—when separate from the end—are less than nothing and vanity. If they do not actually lead to the knowledge and love of God, they are not acceptable in His sight. They are rather an abomination before Him, a stink in His nostrils. He is weary of them. And if they are used to try to fulfill the religion they should only serve, they turn God's arms against Himself and keep Christianity out of the heart instead of being the means by which it is brought in.

praying for mercy

*It does not. . .depend on man's desire or effort,
but on God's mercy.*
ROMANS 9:16 NIV

Salvation by faith is an uncomfortable doctrine to the
self-righteous. The devil speaks like himself (without
either truth or shame) when he declares its discomfort, for
salvation by faith is the only comfortable doctrine, very full
of comfort, to all self-destroyed, self-condemned sinners.
Whoever believes on Him will not be ashamed: And the
same Lord over all is rich unto all that call upon Him. Here
is comfort, high as heaven, stronger than death!

What! Mercy for all? For Zacchaeus, a public robber?
For Mary Magdalene, a common harlot? Then one may
say, "Then I, even I, may hope for mercy!" And so you
may, afflicted one, whom no one has comforted! God will
not cast out your prayer. Perhaps He may say the very next
hour, "Be of good cheer, your sins are forgiven." So forgiven
that they shall reign over you no more. Yes, and the Holy
Spirit will bear witness with your spirit that you are a child
of God.

O glad tidings of great joy, sent unto all people! To
everyone who thirsts, come to the waters: And you who
have no money, come, buy, and eat (see Isaiah 55:1).
Though your sins be red like crimson, though more than
the hairs of your head, return unto the Lord, and He
will have mercy upon you; and to our God, for He will
abundantly pardon.

prayer through temptation

The Lord knows how to rescue the godly from temptation.
2 Peter 2:9 NASB

If darkness is occasioned by manifold, heavy, and unexpected temptations, the best way of removing and preventing this is to teach believers always to expect temptation. They dwell in an evil world, among wicked, subtle, malicious spirits, and have a heart capable of evil. They must be convinced that the whole work of sanctification is not, as they may have imagined, wrought at once. When they first believe, they are as newborn babes who are to gradually grow up. They may expect many storms before they come to the full stature of Christ.

Above all, let them be instructed, when the storm is upon them, not to reason with the devil but to pray. Let them pour out their souls before God and show Him of their trouble. And these are the persons unto whom, chiefly, we are to apply the great and precious promises. Not to the ignorant, till the ignorance is removed. Much less to an impenitent sinner.

To the tempted we may declare the loving-kindness of God. Dwell upon His faithfulness and the virtue of that blood shed for us to cleanse us from all sin. God will bear witness to His Word and bring them out of trouble. He will say, "Arise, shine; for your light has come! And the glory of the Lord is risen upon you."

Indeed, that light, if you walk humbly and closely with God, will shine more and more unto the perfect day (see Proverbs 4:18).

Every new victory which a soul gains is the effect of a new prayer. . . . In the greatest temptations, a single look to Christ, and the barely pronouncing his name, suffices to overcome the wicked one, so it be done with confidence and calmness of spirit.

JOHN WESLEY

jesus' intercession for us

*Let us draw near with a true heart
in full assurance of faith.*
HEBREWS 10:22 NKJV

By that faith in His life, death, and intercession for us, renewed from moment to moment, we are every whit clean. There is not only now no condemnation for us, but no such desert of punishment as was before, the Lord cleansing both our hearts and our lives.

By the same faith, we feel the power of Christ every moment resting upon us, by which alone we are what we are. By this alone, we are enabled to continue in spiritual life. Without this, regardless of all our present holiness, we should be devils the next moment.

But as long as we retain our faith in Him, we draw water out of the wells of salvation. We lean on our beloved, even Christ in us the hope of glory, who dwells in our hearts by faith.

He likewise is interceding for us at the right hand of God; we receive help from Him to think, speak, and act what is acceptable in His sight.

Thus does He go before us in all our doings, so that all our designs, conversations, and actions are begun, continued, and ended in Him.

Thus also does He cleanse the thoughts of our hearts by the inspiration of His Holy Spirit, that we may perfectly love Him, and worthily magnify His holy name.

How are we to wait?

Seek the LORD while he may be found;
call on him while he is near.
ISAIAH 55:6 NIV

Suppose one knows this salvation to be the gift and the work of God, and suppose further that one is convinced also that one does not have this gift, how might one attain to it?

If you say, "Believe, and you will be saved!" they answer, "True, but how shall I believe?" You reply, "Wait upon God."

"Well, but how am I to wait? Using the means of grace, or not? Am I to wait for the grace of God, which brings salvation by using the means of grace, or by laying them aside?"

It cannot be conceived that the Word of God should give no direction in so important a point; or that the Son of God, who came down from heaven for us and for our salvation, should have left us without direction with regard to a question in which our salvation is so nearly concerned. And, in fact, He has *not* left us undirected; He has shown us the way in which we should go. We have only to consult the Word of God. Inquire what is written there. If we simply abide by that, no possible doubt can remain.

According to holy scripture, all who desire the grace of God are to wait for it in the means which He has ordained—*in using, not in laying aside*, prayer; hearing, reading, and meditating on the scriptures; and partaking of the Lord's Supper.

love in the heart

*The love of God has been poured out in our hearts
by the Holy Spirit who was given to us.*
ROMANS 5:5 NKJV

A third scriptural mark of those who are born of God, and the greatest mark of all, is *love*. It is the love of God, which is poured into our hearts by the Holy Spirit when we are born again of the Spirit of God. "Because you are sons," St. Paul wrote to the Galatians, "God has sent forth the Spirit of His Son into your hearts, crying out, 'Abba Father!' " (Galatians 4:6 NKJV). By this Spirit, continually looking up to God as their reconciled and loving Father, they cry to Him for their daily bread, for all things needful, whether for soul or body. They continually pour out their hearts before Him, knowing they have those petitions they ask of Him (see 1 John 5:14–15). Their delight is in Him; He is the joy of their hearts. The desire of their soul is toward Him; it is their great satisfaction to do His will.

They love God as their Savior. They love the Lord Jesus Christ in sincerity. They are so joined unto the Lord as to be one spirit. Their souls hang upon the Lord Jesus and count Him the chief among ten thousand. They know what it means of which the psalmist wrote: "You are fairer than the sons of men; grace is poured upon Your lips; therefore God has blessed You forever" (Psalm 45:2 NKJV).

god is the giver

Every good and perfect gift is. . .from the Father.
JAMES 1:17 NIV

It is true that outward religion is worth nothing without the religion of the heart. "God is a Spirit: and they that worship him must worship him in spirit and in truth" (John 4:24 KJV). Therefore, external worship is lost labor without a heart devoted to God. The outward ordinances of God profit much when they advance inward holiness. But when they do not advance it, they are unprofitable and void. And when they are used in the place of inward religion, they are an utter abomination to the Lord.

All outward means whatever, if separate from the Spirit of God, cannot profit at all, cannot lead in any degree either to the knowledge or the love of God. Without controversy, the help that is done upon earth, He doeth it Himself. It is He alone who, by His own almighty power, works in us what is pleasing in His sight. All outward things, unless He works in them and by them, are mere weak and beggarly elements. We know there is no inherent power in the words spoken in prayer, in the letter or the sound of the scripture read, or in the bread and wine received in the Lord's Supper. It is God alone who is the giver of every good gift, the author of all grace. The whole power is of Him, whereby, through any of these, there is any blessing conveyed to our souls.

prayer and god's promises

*For a little while you may have had to suffer grief
in all kinds of trials.*
1 PETER 1:6 NIV

More especially in time of sickness and pain does Satan press with all his might, "Does not God say, 'Without holiness no one shall see the Lord?' You know holiness is the full image of God, and how far is this out of your sight! You cannot attain unto it. All these things you have suffered in vain. You are yet in your sins, and you must perish at the last."

If your eye is not steadily fixed on Him who has borne all your sins, Satan will again bring you under that fear of death in which you were once subject to bondage. By this means he impairs, if not wholly destroys, your peace as well as joy in the Lord. Now, the peace of God is a precious means of advancing the image of God in us. There is scarcely a greater help to holiness than this—a continual tranquility of spirit, the evenness of a mind fixed upon God, a calm repose in the blood of Jesus.

Without this, it is scarcely possible to grow in grace and in the vital knowledge of our Lord Jesus Christ. So, hold fast the beginning of your confidence steadfast to the end. You shall undoubtedly receive the promise of God, for time and for eternity. Be anxiously careful for nothing. Only make your requests known without doubt or fear but with thanksgiving to the One who has made these precious promises (see Philippians 4:6).

God only requires of his adult children that their hearts be truly purified, and that they offer him continually the wishes and vows that naturally spring from perfect love. For these desires, being the genuine fruits of love, are the most perfect prayers that can spring from it.

JOHN WESLEY

The whole of you

May the God of peace Himself sanctify you entirely.
1 Thessalonians 5:23 NASB

The God of peace sanctifies by the peace which He works in us, which is a great means of sanctification. The word used in the original signifies *wholly and perfectly*—every part and all that concerns us.

And may the whole of you, the apostle continues, *the spirit and the soul and the body, be preserved blameless.* He shows that he wished their spiritual state to be preserved entirely, as well as desiring the health of their natural state.

To explain this a little further: Only the soul and the body are the natural constituent parts of men and women. The *Spirit* is not in the fundamental nature of humans but is the supernatural gift of God, *to be found in Christians only*.

To encourage the Thessalonian Christians, St. Paul added, *Faithful is He who calls you, who also will do it* (v. 24), if you do not quench the Spirit, for which purpose he had already written (v. 19). For wherever the Spirit is, it burns. It flames in holy love, in joy, prayer, thanksgiving.

Oh, quench it not, damp it not in yourself or others, either by neglecting to do good, or by doing evil! As a great means of preventing this, he wrote, *Rejoice evermore; pray without ceasing; in everything give thanks.* A blessed admonition, even in our day!

what is your inward temper?

"They should repent. . .
and prove their repentance by their deeds."
ACTS 26:20 NIV

If the conscience of believers is thoroughly awake, how much sin do they find cleaving to *their actions* also? Indeed, are there not many, whom the world would not condemn, who cannot be commended nor even excused if we judge by the Word of God?

Many of their actions are not to the glory of God; frequently they did not even aim at His glory. Many are doing their own will as least as much as His and seeking to please themselves as much if not more than to please God.

While they are endeavoring to do good to their neighbor, do they not feel wrong tempers of various kinds? Hence, their good actions, their *works of mercy*, are polluted with a mixture of evil. Is it not the same case when they are offering up their prayers to God, public or private, or engaged in the most solemn service? Are not their hearts often wandering to the ends of the earth?

Again, how many *sins of omission* are they chargeable with! We know the words of the apostle James, "To him who knows to do good and does not do it. . .it is sin" (James 4:17 NKJV). And do they not find in themselves a lack of love and holy tempers, and other *inward defects* without number? So that they cry, with Job, "I abhor myself, and *repent in dust and ashes*" (Job 42:6 KJV).

prayer and self-denial

*"He must deny himself and take up
his cross daily and follow me."*
LUKE 9:23 NIV

An understanding of our Lord's meaning of these words is critical. In every stage of the spiritual life, there is a variety of hindrances to attaining grace or growing in it. Yet, all are resolvable into these general ones: Either we do not deny ourselves, or we do not take up our cross.

This is a point most opposed by numerous and powerful enemies. All our nature rises up in its own defense against this. Those who take nature rather than grace for their guide abhor the very sound of it. The great enemy of our souls well knows its importance and moves every stone against it.

Even those who have in some measure shaken off the yoke of the devil and experienced a real work of grace in their hearts are not friends to this grand doctrine of Christianity. Although it is peculiarly insisted on by their Master, some are as deeply ignorant of it as if there were not one word about it in the Bible.

Others are further off still, having unawares imbibed strong prejudices against it. They represent self-denial and taking up our cross in the most odious colors. They call it *seeking salvation by works or seeking to establish our own righteousness*. You are in constant danger of being wheedled, harassed, or ridiculed out of this important gospel doctrine. Let fervent prayer, then, go before, accompany, and follow what you are about to read.

god will do greater things

Do not be foolish, but understand what the Lord's will is.
Ephesians 5:17 niv

The inward kingdom of heaven, set up in the hearts of all who repent and believe the gospel, is righteousness, peace, and joy in the Holy Spirit. But these are only the firstfruits. While these blessings are inconceivably great, yet we trust to see greater.

We trust to love the Lord our God not only as we do now, with a weak though sincere affection, but with all our heart, mind, soul, and strength. Indeed, we expect to be "made perfect in love" (1 John 4:18 nkjv). We look for power to rejoice always, pray without ceasing, and give thanks in everything. We believe the whole mind will be in us that was in Christ Jesus (see Philippians 2:5). And we expect to be cleansed from all our idols and saved from all our uncleannesses, inward or outward (see Ezekiel 36:29)—to be purified, as He is pure.

We look for such an increase in the experiential knowledge and love of God our Savior as will enable us always to walk in the light as He is in the light. We trust in His promise who cannot lie that the time will surely come when all we do shall be done to the glory of God.

The grand device of Satan is to destroy the first work of God in our souls, or at least to hinder its increase, by our expectation of that greater work. Yet there are ways to retort these fiery darts and rise the higher by what he intends for our falling.

the ways of salvation

In the night I remember your name, O LORD,
and I will keep your law.
PSALM 119:55 NIV

It has been already observed that there is an order in which God is generally pleased to use these means as He brings sinners to Himself. Yet we find no command in holy scripture for any particular order to be observed. Neither do the providence and the Spirit of God adhere to any without variation. The means in which different people are led, and in which they find the blessing of God, are varied, transposed, and combined together a thousand different ways.

Yet still our wisdom is to follow the leadings of His providence and His Spirit, more especially as to the means wherein we ourselves seek the grace of God. For He guides us partly by His outward providence, giving us the opportunity of using sometimes one means, sometimes another and partly by our experience whereby His free Spirit is pleased most to work in our hearts.

And in the meantime, the sure and general rule for all who groan for the salvation of God is this: Whenever opportunity serves, use all the means which God has ordained, for who knows in which of them God will meet you with the grace that brings salvation?

Give me one hundred preachers who fear nothing but sin and desire nothing but God, and I care not a straw whether they be clergymen or laymen; such alone will shake the gates of hell and set up the kingdom of heaven on earth.

JOHN WESLEY

waiting on god

With the Lord. . .a thousand years are like a day.
2 PETER 3:8 NIV

If we hold fast, "Other foundation can no man lay than. . . Jesus Christ" and "I am justified freely by God's grace," still Satan urges, "But the tree is known by its fruits; have you the fruits of justification? Is that mind in you which was in Jesus Christ? Are you dead to sin and alive to righteousness?"

And then, comparing the small fruits we feel in our souls with the fullness of the promises, we shall be ready to conclude, "Surely God has not said that my sins are forgiven! Surely I have not received the remission of sins. What lot have I among those who are sanctified?"

But bind this about your neck; write it upon your heart: "I am accepted before God by the righteousness which is of God by faith." Admire more and more the free grace of God in so loving the world as to give His only begotten Son, that whoever believes in Him shall not perish but have everlasting life (see John 3:16). So shall the peace of God flow on in an even stream, in spite of all those mountains of ungodliness. They shall become a plain in the day when the Lord comes to take full possession of your heart. The Lord is not lacking for time to accomplish the work that still needs to be done in your soul. And His time is the best time. Therefore, ask Him and trust in Him, for He cannot withhold from you anything that is good.

The Business of Your Calling

"Do not work for the food which perishes."
JOHN 6:27 NASB

For what *purpose* do you undertake and follow your worldly business? "To provide things necessary for myself and my family." A good enough answer *as far as it goes*, but it does not go far enough for a Christian. We must go abundantly farther. Our purpose in all things is to please God. To do not our own will but the will of God on earth as the angels do in heaven. We work for that which endures to everlasting life.

Again, in what *manner* do you transact your worldly business? I trust with diligence, with all your might. And in justice: rendering to all their due in every circumstance. And in mercy: doing unto everyone as you would they should do to you. But Christians are called to go still farther: to add piety to justice; to intermix prayer—the prayer of the heart—with all the work of their hands. Without this, all the diligence and justice only show them to be honest persons. We must walk a "more excellent way" than honest pagans.

In what *spirit* do you go through your business? In the spirit of the world or in the spirit of Christ? If you act in the spirit of Christ, you do everything in the spirit of sacrifice, giving up your will to the will of God. You continually aim, not at ease, or pleasure, or riches not at anything other than the glory of God. This is the most excellent way of pursuing worldly business!

crying out to the
goodness of god

Shall we go on sinning so that grace may increase?
By no means!
ROMANS 6:1–2 NIV

It may be that some do not speak of the mercy of God saving or justifying us freely by faith because they believe it encourages people in sin. Indeed, it may and will. Many will continue to sin that grace may increase, but their blood is upon their own heads. The goodness of God ought to lead them to repentance, and so it will those who are sincere of heart.

When penitent seekers know there is yet forgiveness with God, they will cry aloud that He would blot out their sins also, through faith which is in Jesus. And if they earnestly cry and faint not, if they seek Him in all the means He has appointed, if they refuse to be comforted till He come, He will come, and will not tarry (Hebrews 10:37). And He can do much work in a short time.

The Acts of the Apostles records many examples of God's working this faith in men's and women's hearts, even like lightning falling from heaven. In the same hour that Paul and Silas began to preach, the jailer repented, believed, and was baptized. It was the same with the three thousand on the day of Pentecost who repented and believed at St. Peter's first preaching. And, blessed be God, there are now many living proofs that God is still "mighty to save."

seeking the Lord and obedience

"To obey is better than sacrifice."
1 Samuel 15:22 NIV

Another passage in which the expression "Stand still" occurs reads thus: "Then some came and told Jehoshaphat, saying, 'A great multitude is coming against you from beyond the sea'. . . . And Jehoshaphat feared, and set himself to seek the Lord, and proclaimed a fast throughout all Judah. So Judah gathered together to ask help from the Lord; and from all the cities of Judah they came to seek the Lord. Then Jehoshaphat stood in the assembly. . .in the house of the Lord. . . . Then the Spirit of the Lord came upon Jahaziel. . .and he said, 'Listen. . .Thus says the Lord to you:

> Do not be afraid nor dismayed because of this great multitude. . . . Tomorrow go down against them. . . . You will not need to fight in this battle. Position yourselves, stand still and see the salvation of the Lord'. . . . So they rose early in the morning and went out. . . . Now when they began to sing and to praise, the Lord set ambushes against the people of Ammon, Moab, and Mount Seir. . .[and] they helped to destroy one another."

2 Chronicles 20:2–23 NKJV

Such was the salvation that the children of Judah saw. They obeyed. *They sang and praised the Lord.* But how does all this prove that we ought not to wait for the grace of God in the means which He has ordained?

WRITTEN OF JOHN WESLEY:

He thought prayer to be more his business than anything else, and I have seen him come out of his closet with a serenity of face next to shining.

Taking Care of the Body

Whether, then, you eat or drink or whatever you do,
do all to the glory of God.
1 CORINTHIANS 10:31 NASB

These "houses of clay" which clothe our spirits require constant reparation, or they will sink into the earth even sooner than nature requires. Daily *food* is necessary to prevent this, to repair the decays of nature. It was common in the heathen world, when they were about to eat, to pour out a little drink to the honor of their god (although the heathen gods were but devils—see 1 Corinthians 10:19–21). There was once just such a common custom in this land. Would it not be a more excellent way if every head of family were to ask a blessing from God on what was about to be eaten and to return thanks to the giver of all blessings?

As to the *quantity* of food, good sorts of people do not usually eat to excess; at least not so as to make themselves sick with food or to intoxicate themselves with drink. As to the manner of eating, it is usually innocent, mixed with a little mirth, which is said to aid digestion. Provided they take only that measure of plain, wholesome food which most promotes health both of body and mind, there will be no cause of blame. Hunger is said to be a "good sauce" for the appetite; but a still better sauce is cheerful thankfulness, and the food so seasoned is the most agreeable kind. You may thus receive every morsel as God's pledge of life eternal.

sing of his love

. . .declares the Lord.
I will put my laws in their minds
and write them on their hearts. . . .
and will remember their sins no more.
HEBREWS 8:10, 12 NIV

After you have used any of these means of grace, take care how you value yourself on them; how you congratulate yourself as having done some great thing. This is turning all into poison. The cause of our redemption is not our own works or righteousness, but the kindness and love of God our Savior. . .according to His mercy. . .that we might become heirs of eternal life (see Titus 3:4–7).

Meantime, think, "If God was not there, what does using this means avail? Have I not been adding sin to sin? O Lord, save, or I perish! O lay not this sin to my charge!"

If God *was* there, if His love flowed into your heart, you have already forgotten the outward work. You see, you know, you feel, God is all in all. Be abased. Sink down before Him. Give Him all the praise. Let God in all things be glorified through Christ Jesus. Cry from the depth of your heart, "My song shall be always of the lovingkindness of the Lord, with my mouth I will ever be telling of Your truth from one generation to another!" (see Psalms 89:1 and 100:5.)

praying for grace

Teach me your way, O Lord;
lead me in a straight path.
PSALM 27:11 NIV

By observing the order in which God leads a sinner, we may learn what means to recommend to any particular soul. If any thing will reach a careless sinner, it is probably hearing, or conversation, if he ever has any thought about salvation. To one who begins to feel the weight of his sins, not only hearing the Word of God, but reading it, too, and perhaps other serious books, might be a means of deeper conviction. He is well advised also to meditate on what he reads that it may have its full force upon his heart. And to speak freely, particularly among those who walk in the same path. When trouble and heaviness take hold upon him, he should then be earnestly exhorted to pour out his soul before God, always to pray and not lose heart. And when he feels the worthlessness of his own prayers, remind him of going up into the house of the Lord, to pray with all who fear Him. But if he does this, the word of his Lord will soon be brought to his remembrance to eat and drink the Lord's Supper.

We should second the motions of the blessed Spirit, for one is thus led, step by step, through all the means God has ordained—not according to our own will, but just as the providence and the Spirit of God go before and open the way.

sustaining spiritual birth

"So is everyone who is born of the Spirit."
JOHN 3:8 NASB

When one is born of God, born of the Spirit, how the manner of his existence is changed! His whole soul is now sensible of God, and he can say, by sure experience, "You are about my bed and about my path."

The Spirit or breath of God is immediately breathed into the newborn soul. The same *breath* that comes from God also returns to God. As it is continually received by faith, so it is continually rendered back by love, prayer, praise, and thanksgiving. Love, prayer, and praise are the breath of every soul that is truly born of God. By these, spiritual life is not only sustained but increased day by day.

The *eyes* of his understanding are now open, seeing the One who is invisible. He clearly perceives the pardoning love of God toward him and all His exceeding great and precious promises. His *ears* are now opened, and the voice of God no longer calls in vain. He knows the voice of his Shepherd—he hears and obeys the heavenly calling.

All his spiritual senses being now awakened, he has a clear communication with the invisible world. He now knows what the peace of God is: joy in the Holy Spirit and the love of God that is poured out in the hearts of those who believe. The veil is removed; there is nothing between the soul and the light, the knowledge and the love of God.

altogether a christian: the love of god

> " 'Love the Lord your God with all your heart.' "
> MATTHEW 22:37 NASB

We come, second, to what is implied in being altogether a Christian.

First, the love of God. So says His Word: " 'You shall love the LORD your God with all your heart, with all your soul, with all your mind, and with all your strength' " (Mark 12:30 NKJV). Such a love as this occupies the whole heart, takes up all the affections, fills the entire capacity of the soul, and employs the utmost extent of all its faculties.

One who thus loves is continually rejoicing in God. His delight is in the Lord, his Lord and his all, to whom he gives thanks in all things. All his desire is toward God and to the remembrance of His name. His heart is always crying out, "Whom have I in heaven but Thee? and there is none on earth that I desire beside Thee."

Indeed, what can he desire but God? Not the world or the things of the world, for he is crucified to the world and the world is crucified to him. He is crucified to the desire of the flesh, the desire of the eye, and the pride of life. He is dead to pride of every kind: For "love is not puffed up." One who is dwelling in love, dwells in God, and God in him; and he is less than nothing in his own eyes. For the love of God is a mark of *the altogether Christian*.

Whether we think of; or speak to, God, whether we act or suffer for Him, all is prayer, when we have no other object than His love and the desire of pleasing Him.

JOHN WESLEY

counting on prayer

*"Not everyone who says to me, 'Lord, Lord,'
will enter the kingdom of heaven."*
MATTHEW 7:21 NIV

Our Lord's expression in this text implies (to begin at the lowest point) all good words, all verbal religion. It includes whatever creeds we may recite, whatever professions of faith we make, whatever numbers of prayers we may repeat, whatever thanksgivings we read or say to God.

We may speak well of His name and declare His lovingkindness to all. We may be talking of all His mighty acts and telling of His salvation from day to day.

By comparing spiritual things with spiritual, we may show the meaning of the Word of God. We may explain the mysteries of the kingdom which have been hid from the beginning of the world.

We may speak with the tongue of angels rather than men concerning the deep things of God. We may proclaim to sinners, "Behold the Lamb of God, who takes away the sin of the world!" (see John 1:29).

Yes, and we may do this with such a measure of the power of God and such demonstration of His Spirit, as to save many souls from death and hide a multitude of sins. Yet it is very possible, all this may be no more than saying, "Lord, Lord." I may have thus successfully preached to others, snatching many souls from hell, yet still drop into it when I am done. *May God have mercy on us all.*

praying for salvation

*The precepts of the LORD are right,
giving joy to the heart.*
PSALM 19:8 NIV

There is a kind of order wherein God Himself is generally pleased to use these means in bringing a sinner to salvation. One goes senselessly on in his own way. God comes upon him unaware—by an awakening sermon or conversation, an awful providence, or a stroke of His convincing Spirit without any outward means. Having now a desire to flee from the wrath of God, he purposely goes to hear how it may be done. If he finds a preacher who speaks to the heart, he is amazed and begins searching the scriptures.

The more he *hears* and *reads*, the more convinced he is; the more he meditates day and night. By these means, the arrows of conviction sink deeper into his soul. He begins to *talk* of the things of God and to *pray* to Him, scarce knowing what to say. Perhaps it is only in "groans which cannot be uttered," perhaps doubting whether the high and lofty God will regard such a sinner as he. So he goes to pray with those who know God, in the congregation. He observes others partaking of the Lord's Supper. He thinks, "Christ has said, 'Do this!' How is it that I do not? I am too great a sinner; I am not worthy."

He struggles awhile, finally breaking through; and so he continues in God's way: *in hearing, reading, meditating, praying, and partaking of the Lord's Supper*; till, in the manner that pleases Him, God speaks, "Your faith has saved you. Go in peace."

Having a Form of Godliness

Having a form of godliness but denying its power.
2 TIMOTHY 3:5 NIV

Those who have the form of godliness do not merely abstain from all outward evil, doing all possible good. They also use the means of grace at all opportunities, especially by attending the house of God as frequently as possible. Nor do they come in looking gaudy and acting impertinent, gazing about with careless indifference. They do not sleep or recline in sleeping posture; nor do they act as though God is asleep, talking with one another or merely seeming to use a prayer to God for his blessing.

No; they behave with seriousness and attention in every part of the solemn service, especially during the Lord's Supper. Theirs is not a careless behavior; but a deportment which says only, "God be merciful to me, a sinner."

If they are heads of families they practice family prayer, and they set aside times also for private addresses to God.

Those who have the form of godliness, being *almost Christians*, have also a real, inward principle of religion, a *sincerity*, from which these outward actions flow. Indeed, without sincerity, one does not have even primitive honesty, for even pagans made a difference between those who avoided sin from fear of punishment and those who did so from a love of virtue. Without the inward principle of sincerity, one is not even *almost a Christian*. He is, rather, only a hypocrite altogether!

Guarding with Prayer

Put on the whole armor of God,
that you may be able to stand.
EPHESIANS 6:11 NKJV

Guard *against wicked spirits* who continually strive to infuse unbelief, pride, idolatry, malice, envy, anger, hatred *in heavenly places*, which were once their dwelling place and which they still aspire to as far as they are permitted. And so we need *the whole armor of God.*

In the evil day (v. 13)—the war is perpetual, but the fight is one day less, another more, violent. *The evil day* is either at the approach of death, or in life. It may be longer or shorter, and admits of numberless varieties.

That you may still keep your armor on and still stand upon your guard, you must still watch and pray. Thus, you will be enabled to endure unto the end and *stand* with joy before the face of the Son of Man at "the last day."

So that you may be ready for every motion, have *your loins girt about with truth*, not only with the truths of the gospel, but with "truth in the inward parts" (Psalm 51:6 NKJV). So our Lord is described (Isaiah 11:5). Without inward truth, all our knowledge of divine truth will prove but a poor "girdle" in *the evil day*. And as a girded man or woman is always ready to go forward, so this seems to indicate an obedient heart and a ready will, the inseparable companions of faith and love.

restrain them from evil

"The Lord disciplines those he loves."
HEBREWS 12:6 NIV

What can we do that all our household may serve the Lord? May we not endeavor, first, to restrain them from all outward sin—from taking the name of God in vain and doing needless work on the Lord's Day? Those you hire may be restrained by argument or persuasion, but if they will not yield, they must be dismissed, be it ever so inconvenient.

Your spouse cannot be dismissed, except for adultery. In other cases, what can be done if *open sin is habitual?* All that can be done is done partly *by example*, partly *by argument or persuasion*, as dictated by Christian prudence. If evil ever can be overcome, it must be by good. We cannot beat the devil with his own weapons. If this evil cannot be overcome by good, we are called to suffer it. When God sees it to be best, He will remove it. Meantime, continue in earnest prayer; in due time, He will either take the temptation away or make it a blessing to your soul.

While your children are young, you may restrain them from evil *by advice, persuasion, and reproof,* and also *by correction.* Only remember, this means is to be used last—after all others have been tried and found ineffectual. All should be done with mildness and with kindness. Otherwise, your own spirit suffers loss and the child reaps little advantage. Only do not think yourself wiser than God. He said, "Chasten. . .while there is hope, and let not thy soul spare for his crying" (Proverbs 19:18 KJV).

Bear up the hands that hang down, by faith and prayer; support the tottering knees. Have you any days of fasting and prayer? Storm the throne of grace and persevere therein, and mercy will come down.

JOHN WESLEY

christ is all

Christ is all, and in all.
COLOSSIANS 3:11 NASB

We know that God is able to give His grace though there were no means on the face of the earth. In this sense, we may affirm that, with regard to God, there is no such thing as means, seeing He is equally able to work whatever pleases Him, by any means, or by none at all.

We know, further, that the use of *all means* whatever will never atone for one sin. It is the blood of Christ alone whereby any sinner can be reconciled to God. There is no other propitiation for our sins, no other fountain for sin and uncleanness.

Every believer in Christ is deeply convinced that there is no merit except in Him. There is no merit in any of their own works: not in uttering the prayer, or searching the scripture, or hearing the Word of God, or eating that bread and drinking of that cup of the Lord's Supper. If those who say, "Christ is the only means of grace," mean that He is the only meritorious cause of grace, it cannot be disputed by any who know the grace of God. For "Christ," as the apostle said, "is all, and in all."

not just saying one's prayers

"Many will say to Me on that day,
'Lord, Lord, did we not prophesy in Your name?'"
MATTHEW 7:22 NASB

Our Lord frequently declared that none who have not the kingdom of God within them shall enter into the kingdom of heaven.

Yet He well knew that many would not receive that saying. So He confirms it yet again: "Many [not one; not a few only; it is not a *rare* thing] will say to Me in that day," not only have we said many prayers; we have spoken Your praise; we have done no evil; but what is much more: "we have prophesied in Your name." We have declared Your will to men and women, we have showed sinners the way to peace and glory. And we have done this "in Your name," according to the truth of Your gospel. In or by Your name, by the power of Your Word and of Your Spirit "have we cast out devils. And in Your name [by Your power, not ours] have we done many miracles."

But Jesus said, "And then I will declare to them, I never knew you"; I never knew you as My own, for your heart was not right toward God. You were not meek and lowly; you were not lovers of God and all mankind. You were not renewed in the image of God; you were not holy as I am holy. "Depart from Me, you" who, in spite of all this, are "workers of lawlessness"—transgressors of My law, My law of holy and perfect love. You have built upon the sand.

prayer as a useful pastime

Let your speech always be with grace.
COLOSSIANS 4:6 NASB

Our times of taking food are usually times of *conversation*. It is natural to refresh our minds while we refresh our bodies. One hopes the subjects of conversation would be harmless, modest, true, and kind, with no talebearing, backbiting, or evil-speaking. But it must also be good: good in itself and on a good subject. You must indeed speak of worldly things, otherwise you may as well go out of this world. But it should be only so far as is needful, then return to a better subject. Secondly, the conversation must be useful to build up either the speaker, the listeners, or both: Lift them up in faith, or love, or holiness. Thirdly, see that it gives not only entertainment, but in one way or another, ministers grace to the hearers. This is "a more excellent way" than mere harmlessness.

But we cannot always be intent upon business; both our minds and bodies require relaxation. Diversions are of various kinds, and which are "more excellent" for a Christian? A diversion may be indifferent in itself yet the surroundings be irreverent, base and vile, or with such a tendency. Even innocent pastimes may be superceded by those which are useful as well as innocent, such as visiting the sick, poor, the widows, and fatherless. Or by the reading of useful subjects and by prayer, the most useful of all pastimes, and indeed "a more excellent way."

all my goods, all my heart

Do all to the glory of God.
1 CORINTHIANS 10:31 NASB

Laying up treasures on earth is as flatly forbidden by our Lord as murder or adultery. By doing so, you are laying up "wrath against the day of wrath and revelation of the righteous judgment of God."

But suppose it were not forbidden? Can you, on principle of reason, spend your money in a way which God may *possibly forgive*, instead of spending it in a manner which He will *certainly reward*? You will have no reward in heaven for what you *lay up*; you will for what you *lay out*. Every dollar you put into the earthly bank is sunk; it brings no interest above. But every dollar you give to the poor is put into the bank of heaven. And it will bring glorious interest, accumulating to all eternity.

Who then is the wise one, endued with knowledge, among you? Let that one resolve this day, this hour, this moment, the Lord assisting him, to choose in all particulars the "more excellent way." And let him or her steadily keep that resolve with regard to sleep, prayer, work, food, conversation, and diversions, but particularly with regard to the employment of that important talent, money. Let *your* heart answer to the call of God, "From this moment, God being my helper, I will lay up no more treasure upon earth. I will lay up treasure in heaven. I will give to God the things that are His: all my goods and all my heart."

TO ACCOMPLISH GOD'S PURPOSE

"I have tested you in the furnace of affliction."
ISAIAH 48:10 NASB

As having an absolute power over the heart of man, God moves all the springs of the heart at His pleasure. In some instances, He causes those whom it pleases Him to go on from strength to strength, even till they "perfect holiness," with scarcely any heaviness at all. But these cases are rare. God generally sees good to try acceptable men and women in the furnace of affliction.

Therefore, manifold temptations and heaviness, more or less, are usually the portion of His dearest children. Indeed, almost all the children of God experience this, in a higher or lower degree.

We ought, doubtless, to watch and pray and use our utmost endeavors to avoid falling into darkness. But we need not care so much how to *avoid* heaviness as how to *improve* ourselves when it comes. Let us be careful to wait upon the Lord so that heaviness may accomplish the end for which He has permitted it—that our faith may be increased, our hope confirmed, unholy tempers purged away, and our love perfected.

Let us earnestly work together with Him, by the grace which He is continually giving us, in "purifying ourselves from all pollution, both of flesh and of spirit." And by daily growing in the grace of our Lord Jesus Christ, till we are received into His everlasting kingdom!

Prayer is certainly the grand means of drawing near to God, and all other means are helpful to us only so far as they are mixed with, or prepare us for, this.

JOHN WESLEY

Real Christianity

Without faith it is impossible to please Him.
HEBREWS 11:6 NASB

If I. . .do not have love, it profits me nothing.
1 CORINTHIANS 13:3 NASB

Some men and women build their hope of salvation upon their innocence. Are you one of these? Do you build upon your doing no harm—not wronging or hurting anyone? You are just in all your dealings. You are downright honest, paying everyone what is due. You neither cheat nor extort; you act fairly with all. And you have a conscience toward God; you do not live in any known sin.

That is all well so far, but still it is not salvation. You may go thus far and yet never come to heaven. When all this harmlessness flows from a right principle, it is *the least part* of the religion of Christ. But if it does not flow from a right principle, it is no part at all of religion. So that in grounding your hope of salvation on this alone, you are still building upon the sand.

Do you go further yet? Do you add to your doing no harm? Observe all the means of grace? At all opportunities, observe the Lord's Supper, use public and private prayer, fast as often as you can, hear and search the scriptures and meditate on them?

True, these things ought to be done. Yet these also are nothing if they are without faith, mercy, and the love of God; holiness of heart; heaven opened in the soul. If you have not these, you have still built upon the sand.

praying before conflict

*"If your brother sins against you,
go and tell him his fault between you and him alone."*
MATTHEW 18:15 NKJV

The most literal way of following this first rule above is the best. If you yourself see or hear a fellow Christian commit undeniable sin—so that it is impossible for you to doubt the fact, then your part is plain. Take the first opportunity of going to him and tell him of his fault between the two of you.

Great care must be taken that this is done in a *right spirit* and a right manner. The success of a reproof greatly depends on the spirit in which it is given. Pray earnestly that it may be done in a lowly spirit and a meek one. For a person cannot otherwise be restored than in a spirit of meekness (see Galatians 6:1).

See also that *the manner* in which you speak is according to the gospel of Christ. Avoid everything in look, gesture, tone of voice that savors of pride or self-sufficiency; anything dogmatic or arrogant; anything approaching disdain, overbearing, or contempt. With equal care, avoid all appearance of anger; railing accusation; any shadow of ill will, bitterness, or sourness of expression. Use the air and language of sweetness as well as gentleness, that all may appear to flow from love in your heart. Yet this sweetness need not hinder your speaking in the most serious and solemn manner. As far as possible, use the very words of the holy Word of God, as under the eye of Him who is coming to judge the living and the dead.

praying in the spirit
of gentleness

Restore him gently.
GALATIANS 6:1 NIV

If any good is done by what is spoken, it is God who does it. Pray that He would guard your heart, enlighten your mind, and direct your tongue to such words as He may please to bless. If one opposes the truth, yet he cannot be brought to the knowledge of it, but by gentleness. Still speak in a spirit of tender love, "which many waters cannot quench." If love is not conquered, it conquers all things. Who can tell the force of love?

> *Love can bow down the stubborn neck,*
> *The stone to flesh convert;*
> *Soften, and melt, and pierce, and break*
> *An adamantine heart.*

If you do not have access to speak to the person, you may do it by a messenger, a common friend in whose prudence and uprightness you can thoroughly confide. To speak in your own person is far better; but this way is better than none. Only beware you do not feign lack of opportunity in order to shun the cross. If you can neither speak yourself nor find a confidential messenger, it only remains to write. There may be some circumstances which make this the most advisable way.

When the person has a warm, impetuous temper, the message may be so introduced and softened in writing as to make it far more tolerable. Many will read the very same words which they could not bear to hear. By adding your name, it is almost the same as speaking in person.

speaking with the lord

"All things are possible with God."
MARK 10:27 NIV

It is such general experience of the children of God wherever they live that, however they differ in other points, they generally agree in this: Although we may "by the Spirit, mortify the deeds of the body," and weaken our enemies day by day, yet *we* cannot drive them out. By all the grace given at justification *we* cannot extirpate them. Though we watch and pray ever so much, *we* cannot wholly cleanse either our hearts or our hands.

Most sure, we cannot, till it please our Lord to speak to our hearts again, to speak the second time, "Be clean!" Then only is the leprosy cleansed. Then only the evil root, the carnal mind, is destroyed, and inbred sin subsists no more.

When, in this sense, we have repented, then we are called to "believe the gospel." This also is to be understood in a peculiar sense, different from that wherein we believed in order to be justified. We are to believe the glad tidings of the great, the full, salvation which God has prepared. Believe that the One who is the brightness of His Father's glory, is "able to save to the uttermost all that come to God through Him." He is able to save you from all the sin that still remains in your heart and to supply whatever is lacking in you. This is impossible with man, but with God-Man, all things are possible.

Perhaps no sin of omission more frequently occasions this than the neglect of prayer.

JOHN WESLEY

keeping watch and praying

Whether you turn to the right or to the left,
your ears will hear a voice behind you, saying,
"This is the way; walk in it."
ISAIAH 30:21 NIV

You see the unquestionable progress from grace to sin. Thus it goes on, from step to step: (1) The divine seed of loving, conquering faith remains in the one who is born of God. "He keeps himself" by the grace of God and "cannot commit sin." (2) A temptation arises; whether from the world, the flesh, or the devil, it matters not. (3) The Spirit of God gives him warning that sin is near and bids him more abundantly watch unto prayer. (4) He gives way, in some degree, to the temptation, which now begins to grow pleasing to him. (5) The Holy Spirit is grieved; his faith is weakened; and his love of God grows cold. (6) The Spirit reproves him more sharply, saying, "This is the way; walk in it." (7) He turns away from the painful voice of God and listens to the pleasing voice of the tempter. (8) Evil desire begins and spreads in his soul till faith and love vanish away.

He is then capable of committing outward sin, the power of the Lord being departed from him.

It is unquestionably true, that one who is born of God, keeping himself, does not, cannot commit sin. Yet if he *does not* "keep himself," he may commit all manner of sin with greediness.

the two great commandments

"'You shall love.'"
MARK 12:30 NASB

Loving the Lord God with all your heart, mind, soul, and strength is the first great branch of Christian righteousness. You shall delight yourself in the Lord your God; seeking and finding all happiness in Him. You shall hear and fulfill His word, "My son, give me your heart." And having given Him your inmost soul to reign there without a rival, you may well cry out in the fullness of your heart, "I will love You, O my Lord, my strength. The Lord IS my strong rock; my Savior, my God, in whom I trust."

The second commandment, the second great branch of Christian righteousness, is closely and inseparably connected with the first: "Love your neighbor as yourself." *"Love"*—embrace with the most tender goodwill, the most earnest and cordial affection, the most inflamed desires of preventing or removing all evil and bringing every possible good. *"Your neighbor"*—not only your friends, kinfolk, or acquaintances; not only the virtuous ones who regard you, who extend or return your kindness, but every person, not excluding those you have never seen or know by name; not excluding those you know to be evil and unthankful, those who despitefully use you. Even those you shall love *"as yourself"* with the same invariable thirst after their happiness. Use the same unwearied care to screen them from whatever might grieve or hurt either their soul or body. This is love.

established to all eternity!

Show this same diligence to the very end.
HEBREWS 6:11 NIV

We confirm a gift of God in our souls by a deeper sense of whatever He has shown us—a greater tenderness of conscience and a sharper sensibility of sin. We now walk with joy and not with fear. We look on pleasure, wealth, praise, all things of the earth, as worth nothing in the clear, steady light of eternal things.

Can *you* say, "You, Lord, are merciful to my unrighteousness; my sins You remember no more?" Then, for the time to come, see that you fly from sin as from the face of a serpent! For how exceeding sinful does it appear to you now!

On the other hand, in how amiable a light do you now see the holy and perfect will of God! *Now*, therefore, labor that it may be fulfilled in you, by you, and upon you! *Now* watch and pray that you may sin no more, that you see and shun the least transgression of His law!

When the sun shines into a dark place, you see the motes you could not see before. Now the Sun of Righteousness shines in your heart, and you see the sins you could not see before. *Now* be zealous to receive more light daily, more of the knowledge and love of God, more of the Spirit of Christ, more of His life, and of the power of His resurrection. *Now* use all you have already attained. So shall you daily increase in holy love till faith is swallowed up in sight and the law of love is established to all eternity!

contrary to the love of god

*"Those whom I love I rebuke. . . .
So be earnest, and repent."*
REVELATION 3:19 NIV

Sooner or later after he is justified, the believer feels *self-will*, a will contrary to the will of God. Now a *will* is an essential part of the nature of every intelligent being, even of our blessed Lord Himself. But His human will was always subject to the will of His Father.

The case with even true believers in Christ is that they frequently find their will more or less exalting itself against the will of God. They fight against this self-will with all their might, and thus they continue in the faith.

But self-will, as well as pride, is a species of *idolatry*. Both are directly contrary to the love of God, as is *the love of the world*. It is true, when one first passes from death unto life, he desires nothing more but God. He can truly say, "There is none upon earth that I desire beside You!"

But it is not always so. If he does not continually watch and pray, he feels not only the love of the world but also *lust* reviving and the assaults of *inordinate affection*. He feels the strongest urges toward loving the creature more than the Creator—be it a child, a parent, a husband, a wife, or a well-beloved friend. To the extent he yields to the desire of earthly things or pleasures, he is prone to forget God. And for this, even the true believer in Christ needs to repent.

Lord, I am no longer my own, but Yours. Put me to what You will, rank me with whom You will. Let be employed by You or laid aside for You, exalted for You or brought low by You. Let me have all things, let me have nothing, I freely and heartily yield all things to Your pleasure and disposal. And now, O glorious and blessed God, Father, Son, and Holy Spirit, You are mine and I am Yours. So be it. Amen.

JOHN WESLEY

Being Altogether a Christian

*The love of God has been poured out within our hearts
through the Holy Spirit who was given to us.*
ROMANS 5:5 NASB

It is not enough to shun evil and do good at all opportunities, nor to seriously use all the means of grace with a sincere design and desire to please God.

The great question remains for each of us: Is the love of God poured out in my heart? Does my heart cry that He is my all? Am I happy in God? Is He my delight? And is it written in my heart that those who love God love their neighbor also?

Go further: Do I believe that Christ loved me and gave Himself for me? Do I have faith in His blood? Do I believe that the Lamb of God has taken away my sins and cast them as a stone into the depth of the sea, giving me redemption through His blood, even the remission of my sins? Does His Spirit testify with my spirit that I am a child of God?

Let no one persuade you to rest short of this prize of your high calling. Cry day and night unto Him who, "while we were without strength, died for the ungodly"; until you know Him in whom you have believed and know that you are indeed *altogether a Christian*.

Then, being justified freely by His grace by the redemption that is in Jesus, you will experience that blessed peace with God through Jesus Christ and know the love of God poured into your heart by the Holy Spirit given unto you!

born from above

Born again, not of corruptible seed but incorruptible,
through the word of God which lives and abides forever.
1 PETER 1:23 NKJV

It does not matter if you have done no harm and do not live in any willful sin. You must go further yet, or you cannot be saved. Even if you also do all the good you can and have improved *all opportunities* of doing good, yet this does not alter the case. Still, you must be born again.

Without this, nothing will do any good to your poor, sinful, polluted soul. You may faithfully go to church and observe the sacraments, say ever so many prayers in private; hear ever so many good sermons; read ever so many good books. Still, "you must be born again." None of these things—nor anything else under heaven—will stand in the place of the new birth to keep you from hell, unless you are born again.

If you have not already experienced this inward work of God, let this be your continual prayer: "Lord, add this to all Your blessings—let me be born again. Deny me not this: Let me be 'born from above.' Take away whatever seems good to You—reputation, fortune, friends, health—only give me this, to be born of the Spirit, to be received among the children of God. Let me be born of the incorruptible seed by the Word of God. And then let me daily 'grow in grace and in the knowledge of our Lord and Savior Jesus Christ!' "

A perplexing question

Each one is tempted when, by his own evil desire,
he is dragged away and enticed.
JAMES 1:14 NIV

Many who are sincere of heart have been frequently perplexed by the questions "Does sin precede or follow the loss of faith? Does a child of God first commit sin, and thereby lose his faith? Or does he lose his faith first, before he can commit sin?"

I answer: Some sin of omission, at least, must necessarily precede the loss of faith—some inward sin. But the loss of faith must precede the committing outward sin.

The more any believer examines his own heart, the more he will be convinced of this: Faith, working by love, excludes both inward and outward sin from a soul watching unto prayer. Even then we are liable to temptation, particularly to the sin that does easily beset us.

If the loving eye of the soul be steadily fixed on God, the temptation soon vanishes away. But if not, we are, as the apostle James speaks (v. 14), *drawn out* of God by our *own desire* and *caught by the bait* of present or promised pleasures. Then that desire, conceived in us, brings forth sin (v. 15). And having, by inward sin, weakened and then destroyed our faith, we are cast headlong into the snare of the devil, so that we may commit any outward sin whatever.

Thou, therefore, watch always, that you may always hear and always obey the voice of God!

the cure: pour out your soul in prayer

Examine yourselves. . .test yourselves.
2 CORINTHIANS 13:5 NIV

Have you forced God to depart from you by giving place to anger? Have you fretted because of the ungodly or been envious against evildoers? Have you been offended against your brothers or sisters in the Lord, looking at a real or imagined sin—so as to sin against the law of love by estranging your heart from them? Look to the Lord that you may renew your strength—that all this sharpness and coldness be done away and love, peace, and joy return, together with a tenderhearted, forgiving spirit.

Have you given way to any foolish desire? to any kind or degree of inordinate, unruly, misplaced affection? How then can the love of God have place in your heart till you put away your idols? It is vain to hope for recovery of His light till you "pluck out the right eye" and cast it from you. Cast out every idol from His sanctuary, and the glory of the Lord shall soon appear.

Perhaps it is the lack of striving, a spiritual sloth that keeps your soul in darkness. You go on in the same even track of outward duties and are content to abide there. Do you wonder that your soul is dead? O stir yourself up before the Lord. Shake yourself from the dust. Wrestle with God for the mighty blessing. Pour out your soul in prayer! Continue with all perseverance! Watch! Awake out of sleep and keep awake, that you not be more and more alienated from the light and life of God.

Hold fast your confidence

"The word of the Lord endures forever."
1 PETER 1:25 NASB

It is far easier to conceive than to express the unspeakable violence with which Satan urges temptation on those who are hungering and thirsting after righteousness. They see in a strong, clear light, on one hand, the desperate wickedness of their own hearts. On the other hand is the unspotted holiness to which they are called in Christ Jesus.

Many times, there is no spirit left in them. They see the depth of their total corruption and alienation from God and the height of the glory of the Holy One, and are ready to give up both faith and hope. They are nearly ready to cast away that very confidence whereby they "can do all things with Christ strengthening" them. Yet through this alone will they receive the promise.

When this assault comes, hold fast, "I know that my Redeemer lives and shall stand at the latter day upon the earth." And "I now have redemption in His blood, even the forgiveness of sins."

Thus, being filled with all peace and joy in believing, press on in the peace and joy of faith to the renewal of your whole soul in the image of the One who created you. Meanwhile, cry continually to God that you will see the prize of your high calling, not as Satan represents it but in its native beauty. Not as something that must be or you will go to hell, but as what may be to lead you to heaven.

On every occasion of uneasiness, we should retire to prayer, that we may give place to the grace and light of God and then form our resolutions, without being in any pain about what success they may have.

JOHN WESLEY

A Desperate Necessity

Casting down. . .every high thing. . .
bringing every thought. . .to the obedience of Christ.
2 Corinthians 10:5 NKJV

An accurate view of the nature of repentance and faith in believers is needful in order to avoid the mischief of the opinion that we have no need for further change. For, "they that are whole need not a physician." If we think we are quite made whole already, there is no room to seek further healing.

On the contrary, a deep conviction that we are not yet whole constrains us to groan for a full deliverance to Him that is mighty to save—to implore that He will:

> *Break off the yoke of inbred sin and fully set my spirit free!*
> *I cannot rest till pure within, till I am wholly lost in Thee.*

An accurate view of *this* repentance and *this* faith, coupled with a deep conviction of our *demerit* and our *guilt*, is absolutely necessary in order to our seeing the true value of the atoning blood. We need such in order to sense that we need this as much after we are justified as we ever did before—to know that:

> *He ever lives above for us to intercede—*
> *His all-atoning love, His precious blood, to plead.*

Lastly, an accurate view of the repentance and faith of believers brings a deep conviction of our utter *helplessness* to retain anything we have received, by which we are brought to magnify *Him*, so that *every* temper, thought, word, and work is brought to the obedience of Christ.

faith was added as a means

The LORD God called to the man.
GENESIS 3:9 NIV

It is not certain that *faith*, even in the general sense of the word, had any place in paradise. It is highly probable, from the account we have in the book of Genesis, that Adam (before he rebelled against God) walked with Him by sight and not by faith.

> *For then his reason's eye was strong and clear,*
> *And (as an eagle can behold the sun)*
> *Might have beheld his Maker's face as near*
> *As th' intellectual angels could have done.*

He was then able to talk with God face-to-face, the One whose face we cannot now see and live. Consequently, Adam had no need of that faith whose work it is to supply the lack of sight.

On the other hand, it is absolutely certain that faith in its particular sense had then no place. For in that particular sense, it necessarily presupposes sin and the wrath of God declared against the sinner. Without these, there is no need of an atonement for sin in order to the sinner's reconciliation with God.

As there was no need of an atonement before the fall, so there was no place for faith in that atonement. For man was pure from every stain of sin; holy as God is holy.

And love, even then, filled his heart and reigned there without a rival. But when love was lost by sin, faith was added, not for its own sake, but as the means of reestablishing the law of love.

communion with god in new birth

Created in Christ Jesus.
EPHESIANS 2:10 NASB

Having been born again from above, one may now be properly said to live. God has quickened him by His Spirit, and he is alive to God through Jesus Christ. He lives a life which the world knows not—a life which is "hid with Christ in God." God is continually breathing upon the soul, as by a kind of spiritual respiration, and the soul is breathing unto God. Grace is descending into the heart, and prayer and praise are ascending to heaven. By this communion between God and himself, this fellowship with the Father and the Son, the life of God in the soul is sustained. The child of God grows up, till he comes to the full measure of the stature of Christ (see Ephesians 4:13).

We see that the nature of the new birth is *that great change which God works in the soul when He brings it to life, raising it from the death of sin to the life of righteousness.* It is the change wrought in the whole soul by the almighty Spirit of God when the soul is created anew in Christ Jesus, renewed after the image of God in righteousness and true holiness (see Ephesians 4:24). The love of the world is changed into the love of God; pride into humility; passion into meekness; hatred, envy, malice into a sincere, tender love for all. In a word, it is the change whereby the earthly, sensual, devilish mind is turned into the mind that was in Christ Jesus. This is the nature of the new birth: "*So is everyone who is born of the Spirit.*"

called to god

Do not be conceited, but fear.
ROMANS 11:20 NASB

God goes before us with the blessings of His goodness. He first loves us and manifests Himself unto us. While we are yet afar off, He calls us to Himself and shines upon our hearts. But if we do not then love Him who first loved us nor hearken to His voice, turn our eye away from Him and not attend to the light which He pours in upon us, His Spirit will not always strive (see Genesis 6:3). He will gradually withdraw and leave us to the darkness of our hearts. He will not continue to breathe into our soul, unless our soul breathes toward Him again, unless we unceasingly return to Him our love, praise, and prayer, the thoughts of our hearts, our words, and works: body, soul, and spirit in a holy, acceptable sacrifice (see Romans 12:1).

Let us learn to follow that direction of the great apostle, "Be not high-minded, but fear." Let us fear sin, more than death or hell. Let us have a jealous (though not painful) fear, lest we should lean to our own deceitful hearts. "Let him that standeth take heed lest he fall." Even he who now stands fast in the grace of God, in the faith that overcometh the world, may fall into inward sin and thereby "make shipwreck of his faith." How easily then will outward sin regain its dominion over him! Watch, therefore, that you may pray without ceasing, at all times, and in all places, pouring out your heart before Him! So shall you always believe, always love, and never commit sin!

God's command to "pray without ceasing" is founded on the necessity we have of His grace to preserve the life of God in the soul, which can no more subsist one moment without it, than the body can without air.

JOHN WESLEY

the life of god in the soul

"Be always on the watch,
and pray that you may be able to escape
all that is about to happen."
LUKE 21:36 NIV

The life of God in the soul of the believer immediately and necessarily implies a continual action of God upon the soul by the inspiration of God's Holy Spirit and a reaction of the soul upon God by an unceasing return of love, prayer, and praise.

From this, we may infer the absolute necessity of this continual reaction of the soul upon God in order to the continuance of the divine life in the soul. It plainly appears that God does not continue to act upon the soul unless the soul continues to react upon God.

It is easy to understand how these children of God, David, Barnabas, and Peter, might be moved from their steadfastness, and yet the great truth of God, declared by the apostle John, remain steadfast and unshaken. They did not keep themselves by the grace of God, which was sufficient for each one. Each fell, step by step, first into negative, inward sin, not "stirring up the gift of God which was in him," not "watching unto prayer," not "pressing on to the mark of the prize for his high calling." He went into positive inward sin, inclining to wickedness in his heart, giving way to some evil desire or temper. Next, he lost his faith, his sight of a pardoning God, and, consequently, his love of God. Being then weak and like any other man, he was capable of committing even outward sin.

Heaviness of soul

Ye are in heaviness.
1 Peter 1:6 KJV

There is a near relationship between the darkness of mind in the wilderness state and heaviness of soul, which is more common among believers. The resemblance is so great that they are frequently confounded together. But they are not equivalent terms; far, far from it. The difference is so wide and essential, as all the children of God need to understand, to prevent them sliding out of heaviness into darkness.

The manner of persons to whom the apostle Peter wrote the above words were believers at that time. He expressly says (v. 5) *you are kept by the power of God through faith unto salvation*. Again (v. 7), he mentions *the trial of their faith*; and yet again (v. 9), he speaks of their *receiving the end of their faith, the salvation of their souls*. So, though they were in heaviness, they were possessed of living faith. Their heaviness did not destroy their faith. Neither did it destroy their peace, which is inseparable from true, living faith. The apostle prays (v. 2) not that *grace and peace* may be *given* them, but that it may be *multiplied*.

They were also full of a *living hope*. For he speaks (v. 3) of their living hope of their inheritance that fadeth not away. In spite of their heaviness, they still retained a hope full of immortality. And they still *rejoiced* (v. 8) *with joy unspeakable and full of glory*. Their heaviness, then, was also consistent both with living hope and inexpressible joy!

A Final Challenge

"That the world may believe that You sent Me."
JOHN 17:21 NASB

O that all who bear the name of Christ would put away evil-speaking, talebearing, and whispering. Let none of them proceed out of your mouth! See that you speak evil of no one; of the absent, speak nothing but good.

If you would be distinguished, let it be by this mark: "They censure no one behind his back." What a blessed effect of this self-denial would we quickly feel in our hearts! How our peace would flow like a river! How the love of God would abound in our own souls while we thus confirm our love to our brothers and sisters! And what effect it would have on all that are united in the name of the Lord Jesus! How brotherly love would continually increase when this grand hindrance of it was removed!

Nor is this all. What an effect might this have even on the wild, unthinking world! How soon they would see in us what they could not find among all the thousands of their own, and cry, "See how these Christians love one another!"

By this chiefly would God convince the world and prepare them also for His kingdom. As we may learn from those remarkable words in our Lord's last, solemn prayer: "I pray for those who will believe in Me, that they may be one. . .that the world may believe that You sent Me." *Lord, hasten the time that we thus love one another in deed and in truth, even as Christ has loved us!*

about john wesley

*I have so much to do that I
spend several hours in prayer
before I am able to do it.*

JOHN WESLEY

Short though he was, the Reverend John Wesley stands head and shoulders above others of his time. God used John and his hymn-writing brother Charles to shake England with the scriptural, evangelical truths of grace, faith, repentance, justification, and sanctification. A revival of major proportion spilled out of London into thousands of hamlets, towns, and cities throughout the British Isles, even across the Atlantic to the American colonies.

John Wesley was born in 1703 in Epworth, Lincolnshire, into the large family of an Anglican clergyman. He was educated at Oxford and ordained to the Anglican priesthood. On a missionary voyage to Georgia, he met some German Moravians, by whose piety and simple, steadfast faith he was deeply impressed. When he returned to London, he was helped greatly by a Moravian, Peter Böhler, and in 1738 John reported his "heart strangely warmed" while someone was reading from Martin Luther's "Preface to Romans." He said he then knew that God had, for Christ's sake, forgiven his sins.

He immediately began preaching with a new fervor, and soon the pulpits of the Church of England were closed to him. Encouraged by the Reverend George Whitefield, he began "field preaching," thus reaching the most neglected classes of English society. His listeners often numbered in the thousands;

crowds of 30,000 were reported more than once.

For more than fifty years, Wesley went up and down England and Wales and into Scotland and made numerous voyages across the Irish Sea to Ireland. He preached the gospel unceasingly and wrote voluminously; he also organized believers and inquirers into "societies." These societies were visited in "circuit" by Mr. Wesley, or by those itinerant preachers appointed by and associated with him in the work. Later, after his death, these societies became the backbone of the infant Methodist Church.

The Wesleyan revival drew its power from John's and Charles's emphasis in sermon and song upon an "experimental" (we would say experiential) living faith. John repeatedly spoke and wrote of the "faith that worketh by love," which produced a changed heart and life: inward and outward holiness. Although he responded incisively to critics whenever his preaching was attacked in the press, John Wesley did not concern himself with philosophical or speculative theology. He was too busy warning people to "flee from the wrath to come" and urging them to follow after perfect love—loving God with all their heart, mind, soul, and strength.

John Wesley died in London in 1791. Having murmured, "God be merciful to me a sinner," he passed into his Master's presence crying, "Best of all, God is with us."